JASBO BROWN
AND
SELECTED POEMS

by DuBose Heyward

SKYLINES AND HORIZONS

PORGY

ANGEL

MAMBA'S DAUGHTERS

THE HALF PINT FLASK

BRASS ANKLE
a play

JASBO BROWN AND
SELECTED POEMS

with Hervey Allen
CAROLINA CHANSONS

with Dorothy Heyward
PORGY
(a play)

JASBO BROWN

AND SELECTED POEMS

BY

DuBOSE HEYWARD

FARRAR & RINEHART

INCORPORATED

ON MURRAY HILL, NEW YORK

For permission to reprint certain of these poems, thanks are due to *The London Mercury, The Atlantic Monthly, The North American Review, The Outlook, The Bookman, Poetry: A Magazine of Verse, Contemporary Verse, Voices, Lyric, The Reviewer, The American Mercury* and the *Poetry Society of South Carolina.*

COPYRIGHT, 1924, 1931, BY DuBOSE HEYWARD
PRINTED IN THE UNITED STATES OF AMERICA
BY J. J. LITTLE & IVES COMPANY, NEW YORK
ALL RIGHTS RESERVED

CONTENTS

5

HORIZONS

OTHER POEMS

NEGRO POEMS

JASBO BROWN *

Loose heady laughter shook the humid night,
Bells jangled shrilly, and a whistle flung
A note as lonely as a soul in flight
To fail and die along a mile of river.
Then silence, while a presence moved among
The floating stars and made them swirl and quiver.

Clang-clang! A sudden world swam into view,
Dim windows banked in tiers against the dark,
And paddles threshing phosphorescent blue
Out of abysmal night; tall funnels wreathing
The scene in deeper gloom from their dark
        breathing.

Twin eyes of red and green sought out the shore,
Found it, and centered on the sagging pier.
A sleepy negro woke and raised a cheer.
A painter slapped the planks, and someone swore.

* According to tradition, jazz has taken its name from Jasbo
Brown, an itinerant Negro player along the Mississippi, and
later, in Chicago cabarets.

9

Out of the gloom the shore-line seemed to stir
And swim to greet the phantom visitor.
"Ahoy! Stand by!" Lithe, fluid shadows massed
Upon the wharf. The gang-plank rattled down.
Faint lights came running from the river town.
A door banged open on the boat and cast
An orange glare across the crowded deck,
Gashing the screen of night, secretive, vast,

And showing life, gregarious and teeming,
Bronze torsos under tatters, ridged and gleaming,
Bandanaed heads, a banjo's round blank face.
A woman's voice shrilled "Honey, I's come home."
And from the wharf: "T'ank Gawd! I's glad yo'
    come."
             I got a song, yo' got a song,
             All Gawd' chillen got a song.
Up the plank they trooped a hundred strong,
Throats belling in the warm, moist river air.
Hot laughter on the wharf, the flow and fusion
Of reds and greens and purples, then a flare
Of ecstasy that unified confusion.
"Eberybody talk about Heaben aint goin' dere,
  Heaben, Heaben, goin' sing all ober Gawd'
      Heaben."

From the high pilot house a voice drawled down:
"Got all your niggers off?"
                                    And from below:
"Ay, ay, sir, let her go."
The gang-plank rattled up against its spars.
The tide with ponderous deliberation
Swung out the boat and drew it down the night
To lose it like a fading constellation
Destined for the graveyard of the stars.

Jasbo reeled slightly as he turned to face
The clustered lights that marked the river town.
"Gawd, I's tired," he said, and then far down
Among the shacks: "Heaben, Heaben,"

He raised his head; so, he was not alone.
The chorus throbbed in his deep baritone:
"Goin' sing all ober Gawd' Heaben,"
But no one answered. Yes, that was their way.
He ought to know by now they'd make him play
Out on the river clean from New Orleans,
But in the town they'd drop him mighty quick.
Churches were no place for muddy jeans.
He was not good enough for city ways,
And songs about their Jesus and his grace.

11

No, he was not. He knew it. When they whined
Their mournful hymns a trigger in his mind
Would click, and he would yearn to shout
Queer broken measures that his soul flung out
Of some recess where joy and agony
Whirled in a rhythm that he could feel and see.

The river clucked and sobbed among its piles.
A screech-owl launched a wavering ghost of sound
That ranged and circled on the watery miles
And lived to shudder in the heavy air,
Causing the lonely man upon the pier
To turn and look behind him, while his eyes
Widened and whitened. "Gawd it's lonely here."

He drew a sleeve across his sweating brow.
"All Gawd's chillen got a song," I wonder now—
That girl in New Orleans who sent him packing
Because he had to stroke the ivories
To ease the smart
That always kept devouring his heart,
Instead of heaving cotton on the boat
And earning money for her like the rest.
The sudden thought of her caught at his throat.
Old fires seared him, set his temples throbbing.
"Oh Gawd, I got de blues," he said, half sobbing.

12

Then, suddenly, he heard it down the shore.
A square of light leaped out, and through the
    door
A tinny clamor smote the heavy night.
Someone sang drunkenly, and then a fight
Flamed up and died. The door went BANG.
Something inside of Jasbo broke and sang.

They saw him reel against a shrunken moon
That hung behind him in the open door.
Scarcely at all he seemed a human being,
Lips hanging loosely and his eyes not seeing.
"My Gawd!" a woman cried, "It's Jasbo Brown,
Git off dat stool yo' empty-headed fool
An' let him play what kin."

                    Somebody poured a gin,
Another, and another.
He gulped the liquid fire scarcely knowing,
Lunged heavily and slumped above the keys.
Out of the night a little wind came blowing,
A little wind, and searing memories.
"Oh Gawd, I's lonely," he moaned once, "but
    what's de use!"
Then crashed an aching chord and sang "I got de
    blues."

Oh the hypocritical
Children of the Lord,
How he jeered and mocked them
In a snarling chord.

Women who had known him,
Who had passed him by,
Once again he loved them,
Spurned them, let them die.

Bosses who had cursed him
Over Christendom
Whimpered as he flung them
Into Kingdom Come.

Out of clinkered torment
Like a rising steam,
Something spun and glittered,
Waked him, let him dream.

Showed the world, a madness
Cured by ridicule,
Praised him for a prophet,
Damned him for a fool.

Fingers conjured music
From the ivories

Into swaying bodies,
Into flexing knees.

Black face, brown face,
In the smoky light,
Gin and river women,
And the reeling night

Whirled along a rhythm
Crashing through his blood,
Jasbo, ginned and dreaming,
Stained with river mud.

Dawn, and the music tinkled out and died.
"Jus' one more Jas, here take another gin."
Two dancers dropped and sprawled,
A third stood watching with an empty grin.
The door blew open and the day smiled in.
White-footed down the river it came striding,
Beauty upon it, ancient and abiding,
Breathing of April and of jessamine.
The player rose and staggered to the street.
Oh for a place to go, a hole for hiding.

She came and stood beside him in the dew.
They watched the copper sun swing up together.

"Honey," she said at last, "I'd die for you
Most anytime yo' say when yo' are playin'."
"Yo' likes my songs?" he asked, "Dat what yo're
    sayin'?"
The wonder in her eyes left little doubt.
"Come home with me an' rest. Yo're clean wore
    out."

Down the littered street the player stumbled
With the girl beside him. Once she glanced
Up into his face and found it tranced.
His eyes had lost her, and his loose lips mumbled.
Presently, half aloud, she heard him sing
A low-keyed, minor thing:

> "Yo' got to know
>   I aint de kin' for stayin'
> Always I is movin',
> Always playin'.

> "Life is jus' hello
> An' so-long
> For Gawd's lonely Chillen
> What got a song.

> "Take me home an' res' me
> In de white folks' town.

"But I got to leabe yo'
When de boat comes down.

"De boat, an' de niggers
What love my song.
Life is jus' hello
An' so-long."

PHILOSOPHER

They fight your battles for you every day,
The zealous ones, who sorrow in your life.
Undaunted by a century of strife,
With urgent fingers still they point the way
To drawing rooms, in decorous array,
And moral Heavens where no casual wife
May share your lot; where dice and ready knife
Are barred; and feet are silent when you pray.

But you have music in your shuffling feet,
And spirituals for a lenient Lord,
Who lets you sing your promises away.
You hold your sunny corner of the street,
And pluck deep beauty from a banjo chord:
Philosopher whose future is today.

GAMESTERS ALL

The river boat had loitered down its way;
The ropes were coiled, and business for the day
Was done. The cruel noon closed down
And cupped the town.
Stray voices called across the blinding heat,
Then drifted off to shadowy retreat
Among the sheds.
The waters of the bay
Sucked away
In tepid swirls, as listless as the day.
Silence closed about me, like a wall,
Final and obstinate as death.
Until I longed to break it with a call,
Or barter life for one deep, windy breath.

A mellow laugh came rippling
Across the stagnant air,
Lifting it into little waves of life.
Then, true and clear,
I caught a snatch of harmony;

Sure lilting tenor, and a drowsing bass,
Elusive chords to weave and interlace,
And poignant little minors, broken short,
Like robins calling June —
And then the tune:
"Oh, nobody knows when de Lord is goin' ter
    call,
Roll dem bones.
It may be in de Winter time, and may be in de
    Fall,
Roll dem bones.
But yo' got ter leabe yo' baby and yo' home an
    all—
So roll dem bones,
Oh my brudder,
Oh my brudder,
Oh my brudder,
Roll dem bones!"

There they squatted, gambling away
Their meagre pay;
Fatalists all.
I heard the muted fall
Of dice, then the assured,
Retrieving sweep of hand on roughened board.

I thought it good to see
Four lives so free
From care, so indolently sure of each tomorrow,
And hearts attuned to sing away a sorrow.

Then, like a shot
Out of the hot
Still air, I heard a call:
"Throw up your hands! I've got you all!
It's thirty days for craps.
Come, Tony, Paul!
Now, Joe, don't be a fool!
I've got you cool."

I saw Joe's eyes, and knew he'd never go.
Not Joe, the swiftest hand in River Bow!
Springing from where he sat, straight, cleanly
    made,
He soared, a leaping shadow from the shade
With fifty feet to go.
It was the stiffest hand he ever played.
To win the corner meant
Deep, sweet content
Among his laughing kind;
To lose, to suffer blind,
Degrading slavery upon "the gang,"

With killing suns, and fever-ridden nights
Behind relentless bars
Of prison cars.

He hung a breathless second in the sun,
The staring road before him. Then, like one
Who stakes his all, and has a gamester's heart,
His laughter flashed.
He lunged—I gave a start.
God! What a man!
The massive shoulders hunched, and as he ran
With head bent low, and splendid length of limb,
I almost felt the beat
Of passionate life that surged in him
And winged his spurning feet.

And then my eyes went dim.
The Marshal's gun was out.
I saw the grim
Short barrel, and his face
Aflame with the excitement of the chase.
He was an honest sportsman, as they go.
He never shot a doe,
Or spotted fawn,
Or partridge on the ground.
And, as for Joe,

He'd wait until he had a yard to go.
Then, if he missed, he'd laugh and call it square.
My gaze leapt to the corner—waited there.
And now an arm would reach it I saw hope flare
Across the runner's face.

Then, like a pang
In my own heart,
The pistol rang.

The form I watched soared forward, spun the
     curve.
"By God, you've missed!"
The Marshal shook his head.
No, there he lay, face downward in the road.
"I reckon he was dead
Before he hit the ground,"
The Marshal said.
"Just once, at fifty feet,
A moving target too.
That's just about as good
As any man could do!
A little tough;
But, since he ran,
I call it fair enough."

He mopped his head, and started down the road.
The silence eddied round him, turned and flowed
Slowly back and pressed against the ears.
Until unnumbered flies set it to droning,
And, down the heat, I heard a woman moaning.

PORGY

Porgy, Maria, and Bess,
Robbins, and Peter, and Crown;
Life was a three-stringed harp
Brought from the woods to town.

Marvelous tunes you rang
From passion, and death, and birth,
You who had laughed and wept
On the warm, brown lap of the earth.

Now in your untried hands
An instrument, terrible, new,
Is thrust by a master who frowns,
Demanding strange songs of you.

God of the White and Black,
Grant us great hearts on the way
That we may understand
Until you have learned to play.

SKYLINES

Poems written in the shadow of the Great Smokies

A YOKE OF STEERS

A heave of mighty shoulders to the yoke,
Square, patient heads, and flaring sweep of horn;
The darkness swirling down beneath their feet
Where sleeping valleys stir, and feel the dawn;
Uncouth and primal, on and up they sway,
Taking the summit in a drench of day.
The night-winds volley upward bitter-sweet,
And the dew shatters to a rainbow spray
Under the slow-moving, cloven feet.

There is a power here that grips the mind;
A force repressed and inarticulate,
Slow as the swing of centuries, as blind
As destiny, and as deliberate.

They will arrive in their appointed hour
Unhurried by the goad of lesser wills,
Bearing vast burdens on.
                    They are the great
Unconquerable spirit of these hills.

29

THE WOMAN

Among the sullen peaks she stood at bay
And paid life's hard account from her small store.
Knowing the code of mountain wives, she bore
The burden of the days without a sigh;
And, sharp against the somber winter sky,
I saw her drive her steers afield each day.

Hers was the hand that sunk the furrows deep
Across the rocky, grudging southern slope.
At first youth left her face, and later, hope;
Yet through each mocking spring and barren fall,
She reared her lusty brood, and gave them all
That gladder wives and mothers love to keep.

And when the sheriff shot her eldest son
Beside his still, so well she knew her part,
She gave no healing tears to ease her heart;
But took the blow upstanding, with her eyes
As drear and bitter as the winter skies.
Seeing her then, I thought that she had won.

But yesterday her man returned too soon
And found her tending, with a reverent touch,
One scarlet bloom; and, having drunk too much,
He snatched its flame and quenched it in the dirt.
Then, like a creature with a mortal hurt,
She fell, and wept away the afternoon.

THE GIRL

Life ripens swiftly in these lonely hills,
Ripens, then hangs long-withered on the bough.
Out of their ancient hates, relentless wills,
And unsaid loves, youth burgeons fierce and
    strong,
Ready for life when life has scarce begun;
Eager to spend its all and then be done.

So, as I gaze at Dorothea now,
Wind-blown against the cabin's weathered side,
Defiant, flushed, with bodice blowing wide,
And rain-soaked homespun skirt that cannot hide
The bold, strong, ardent curves of womanhood;
My exultation winces into pain.

Youth, splendid, careless, racing with the rain,
Laughing against the storm as it shouts by.
And yet, perhaps when I pass here again,
Hid from the beat of weathers, she will be
One of the sunken, burned-out lives I see
Here where the mountains shoulder to the sky.

So, as the storm goes smashing down the range,
Striking white fire from the smitten hills,
Swelling the falls and streams until it fills
The cove with giant's music, wild and strange,
The laugh she sends across the shaken air
Brings sudden tears; its very triumph sings
Of beauty so intense it cannot last
Beyond the transient day of fragile things
That brush us, like a wind from unseen wings,
And then are gathered up into the past.

THE PREACHER

In the red church with checkered window-panes,
That squats among its cluttered graves, and stains
The laurelled clearing with its ugly blot,
He preached his God on Sunday, while the hot
Thin mountain air vibrated to the sound
Of hotter threats, and in from miles around,
Threading still trails through rhododendron
    gloom,
Came silent groups to fill his house of doom.

Raw-boned and thunder-voiced, with brandished
    fist,
He shouted of an arrant egotist
Swift to avenge a wrong, carrying hate
Beyond the grave, hurling a dire fate
On all who failed to follow his decree.
Until his God emerged, the Deity
Behind the mountain feud—the iron code
Of eye for eye was His. Slowly there showed,
Behind impassive faces, sullen fear
Of the all-seeing Foe they worshipped there.

Wednesday the freshet came; and Pigeon Creek,
That threads the laurel blossoms on a streak
Of morning sunshine, dropped its slender song,
Drew one deep breath, then lifting with a long
Slow shudder, hurtled like a tawny beast,
Froth-lipped and baying, oceanward and east.
Where the trail leads from church to Garvin's
    house,
Tom Garvin's boy was driving up the cows.
A vaulting seethe of water, trees, and foam
Lunged for the bank, then curved and tumbled
    home.
On yellow chaos, and the sky's hard slate,
For one swift heart-beat, beauty, slim and straight,
Swung sharply upward, crumpled, hung and fell:
There may have been a cry—no one could tell.

That night, ten miles away, the preacher heard.
The first stream took his horse and rig; the third
Hurled him a mile down stream and gashed his
    head.
A sallow morning light lay on the bed
At Garvin's when he staggered through the door
And closed it very softly on the roar
Of hungry water. Slowly silence grew

And spread—and suddenly the watchers knew
There was a God, and He was very kind.
While the grim, silent man, with eyes gone blind,
Gathered the broken form that never stirred
Into his bleeding arms—and said no word.

THE BLOCKADER *

He stands, the symbol of the things that were,
When he, and Daniel Boone, first claimed
  these hills.
Plying his ancient trade above the stir
Of spreading life, the agony of mills,
While demagogues herd cattle to the poll
To break old promises, and while we see
Stout fibres slacken; in his stubborn soul
Beats the old, blind desire to be free.

Into the wilderness among the first
He came. His bloody foot-prints stained the
  snow
At Valley Forge. And always like a thirst,
Freedom to think and do, to come and go,
Burned in his throat. Unsatisfied with named
And labelled variants of liberty,

* The old mountain distiller, whose fight has been for the
principle of personal liberty, has always referred to himself as
a "Blockader." He is not to be confused with the post-Volstead
"moonshiner."

He kept the stinging essence unashamed;
Lived, and let live; or died, if that need be.

Behind the granite ramparts of a land
That no one wanted, still a pioneer,
He broke the forests, fighting hand to hand.
Then built a home, and hung his rifle there.
The German knew him, Mexico, and Spain,
Clear-eyed, untiring, and gaunt. He cares
As little for the revenue. It's plain
He's much too primitive for splitting hairs.

Who knows, but when the slate is clean again,
And wiser generations mock our age;
When force is spent to free, not shackle, *men*,
And youth has claimed its ancient heritage;
Up from the cities, eager pioneers
Will come invading his old fastnesses,
And find his children's sons·the sturdy heirs
Of the unchanging, deathless verities.

THE GRAVEYARD

High on the mountain where the storm-heads are,
Lying where all may see, there is a place
As hideous and shocking as a scar
That mars the beauty of a well-loved face.
Infinitely drear, and raw, and nude,
It waits and listens in the solitude.

There is no friendly tree in all that square
Of scattered stones, and arid, troubled clay.
Bleak as the creed of those who journey there,
Hard as the code by which they lived their day,
It gives them all they ask of it—its best;
No beauty and no softness—only rest.

But oh, the pity of it all is this:
They lived with beauty and their eyes were
    blind.
Dreaming far strong joys, they came to miss
Those that were near. So at the last we find
No tenderness of blossom, but instead
Mute emblems of the longings of the dead.

These rain-bleached sea-shells in an ordered row
Tell of an ocean that they never knew
Except in dreams which, through the ebb and
    flow
Of years, set seaward as the torrents do.
Always they planned to follow, knowing deep
Within their hearts that dreams are but for
    sleep.

And see these tawdry bits of broken glass
Which speak the foreign glories of the town—
The crowds, the lights; these, too, are dreams
    that pass
Here where the hemming walls of rock look
    down,
And clasp their children fast within their keep
Until they cradle them at last to sleep.

Yet all the while, if they could only know
The beauty that is theirs to breathe and touch—
The whisper of the dawn across the snow,
The vast, low-drifting clouds that love them
    much—
Oh, they could call their dreams home down the
    sky,
And carry beauty with them when they die.

BLACK CHRISTMAS

"It is cruel for a woman with her man gone,
An' the younguns allus hungry, an' winter comin'
on."

I thought the feud was ended last Christmas Day,
When Darrell sent the preacher to the Galloways
    to say
That they could come and get him, if they had a
    mind:
He was done with rifle-totin' for his fellow-kind.
An' a year gone by, with everythin' *thet still;*
An' never once a Galloway on our side the hill.
Oh I was glad this mornin' when Dal hollered up
    to me
To sen' the younguns runnin' to help him fetch a
    tree.
"There's a fine young balsam by the wood-house
    shed,
An' we'll have it in for Christmas, like we used to
    do!" he said.
I watched him drop the saplin' with a single stroke;

An' the snow all whirlin' round him like a shinin'
    smoke;
While the younguns tumbled, and laughed, and
    sang:
Then someone shouted sudden—an' a rifle rang.
Now the folks are gatherin' to bring him from the
    shed;
An' I got to stop denyin' that my man is dead.

"It is cruel for a woman with her man gone,
An' the younguns allus hungry, an' winter comin'
    on."

THE TOWN IN SPRING

These are the days when I can love the town;
Now, when the year is clean and new and sweet.
When the great mountain schooners rumble
    down,
White-crested, and slow-moving, fleet on fleet,
Leading a spotted heifer, or a steer,
A rangy mule or two, a pair of hounds;
To barter for a flowered calico,
A ribbon for the red-cheeked daughter's hair,
And black tobacco for the coming year.
Now there is laughter in the open square,
The whine of brakes, and cracking of the whips,
Loud banter while the old horse-trader's mare
Is auctioned—old songs vie with older quips.
The girls go flocking up and down the street,
A startled wonder in their hill-blue eyes,
Amazement and delight upon their lips.
Men, seeming much too large for crowding
    walls,
Stride down the street, and answer with a hail

The greetings of acquaintances they meet.
Boys strut the pavement in new overalls,
And trade unendingly in dogs and guns;
While wagon-hoods frame wan, madonna faces,
That quiver into eager, fleeting smiles,
And there is talk of undiscovered places
Above the soaring laurel-bordered miles.
Soon flame-azaleas on the mountain-side
Will smolder out and die; the laurel-tide
Will sway and hesitate at Summer's touch.
Then they will pass, these people that I know,
And understand a little, and love much.

I STUMBLED UPON HAPPINESS

I stumbled upon happiness once
In a forgotten cove
Between impassable ranges.

With eyes the color of great altitudes
The woman regarded me
Coolly, dispassionately,
A lost Martian dropped upon her world;
Then, with a sudden surge,
Power, vast, inexhaustible,
Swept visibly upward,
Lifted and half-turned
The splendid young torso,
Ridged, stiffened, and bunched
In the clean, straight span of the shoul-
        ders;
Then swung her from me
Down the raw wound of the furrow,
One with the rhythm
That swayed in the heave of her oxen.

Then came the man,
Half of a tree on his shoulder,
And the peace of a nescience,
Wide and abysmal,
Like naked sunlight upon him.

Earth had her way with these two.
Freed of her old weary combat with spirit.
She had modelled this beautiful flesh,
Then tuned it to beat with her rhythms;
Oxen, soil, seed, and human,
In her old perfect cycle.
And for joy, she had given
Strength to sunder, and conquer,
And take, in the sunlight;
And the deep solace to be had
At the hands of a mate
In the hour of shadows.

I looked upon Egypt
Before the first pyramid
Chained flesh to a vision—
Flesh, untrammelled, resilient,
Free from erosion of spirit.

"Philosophy—ethics—art"
He formed the words after me,

46

Tasting their strangeness.
"No such in these mountains."

I stumbled upon happiness once
In the eyes of a man and a woman
In a forgotten cove
Between impassable ranges.

EVENING IN THE GREAT SMOKIES

This is their moment, when the brimming skies
Tilt mellow radiance along the wind
To pour through drowsy valleys, and behind
Far peaks. Compassionate the mountains rise,
Dim with the wistful dimness of old eyes
That, having looked on life time out of mind
Know that the simple gift of being kind
Is greater than all wisdom of the wise.

In this deep moment, hushed and intimate,
When the great hills lean close and understand,
While silence broods, and beauty is made plain,
Children in life's dark house may swing a gate
That lets into a lucent, ample land
Where lips struck dumb may learn to sing again.

HORIZONS

Poems written in the South Carolina Low Country

HORIZONS

This sun-drugged land of ours,
Huge, tawny-limbed, low-breasted like a man,
Sprawling in indolence among sea-nurtured
    flowers,
Dreaming a dream that started
When the first dawn began;
Impersonal as lust,
As fiercely taking;
Holding us until the last
Sharp awful breaking,
Then closing sleepy fingers on our dust.

Why should we give it all!
Why should we bring
Swift pulses, shackled dreams,
White early love!
Wall beyond lifted wall
The Andes swing
Their tilted beauty.
Still Gobi and Sahara pale and flare.

51

Alaskan stars on snow
Call bitter-clear.
And one may know
The transient solace of old, chiseled stone,
And many a girl Madonna,
Many a saint,
Fixed for a heart-beat in a square of paint.

I have said, "I will go.
Another sun will see me freed
Of this old torrid passion.
But, for tonight, I have a need
To rest on warm brown sand,
And watch the slow
Dark breaker of the night
Gather and grow,
Topple against the west,
Then break, and race
Under its spray of stars
To beach on space;
Leaving the east behind it
Washed and white."

Then, while I lie, resolved,
And wait for day;
Across the low-hung moon

Late curlews sway
The trailing pennant
Of their silent flight.
Slowly they curve,
And then come streaming back
Across the yellow disc,
Low on the water like a riding-light,
Then out to sea along the copper track.

That only—nothing more:
Late curlews—and a later moon.
Yet, when the sun
Calls the blue heron out to wade the
     creek,
While alligators boom a sunrise gun
In the dark swamp,
And many-tongued, the waking marshes speak;
I know again that I have been undone.

Undone!
          To dream a whirl of years away
Beneath their tireless spin of suns and moons,
To feel my body drinking, deep and free,
Of sky that knows no trammels but the sea:
And a low range of far tide-bitten dunes.

Undone!

      To stumble on a vacant shore
That has been busy with its urgent life,
And given of its wealth to taking hands.
And watch the sea returning for its own,
Trampling earth ramparts into fluid sands,
Heaping a forest skyward, bone on bone,
Until the equinox shall sweep it bare.

Undone!

      To feel immensity bend near
And lay its weight on me;
While wind, clean from another sphere,
Blows by like pitying laughter.
Then silence—aching—long—
And after,
The raw irony
Of spending soul and brain upon a song.

Undone!

      And yet I know that I shall stay;
Asking but life outside of city walls,
Tides and savannas,
And the aimless sway
Of far curlews,
A solitary heron voyaging south,

54

The ocean's wide, innumerable blues,
And the sweet bitterness
Of salt upon my mouth.
For these are life,
And when they pass from me,
Leaving me stricken and uncomforted,
Although I still may hold the avid ground
Beneath my feet, and thrill to sight and sound,
I shall most surely know that I am dead.

DUSK IN THE LOW COUNTRY

A league of broomstraw, rose, and mauve, and
    umber,
Gashed by a road into the setting sun.
Three heavy-laden cars that groan and lumber
Towards the woods, then vanish one by one.

A line of scarlet and a blur of madder
Behind the trees, the resting earth exhales
Warm humid dusk, and infinitely sadder
Than death or birth, a lone marsh creature wails.

Land of wide beauty and eternal waiting,
You have made loneliness a thing to seek.
How small our loving seems, how little hating,
How less than dust the scattered words we speak.

Here where the aeons pass, and seasons flutter
Like sun and shade across your ample breast,
Your silence thunders down the songs I utter
Who came to be your singer and your guest.

Written at Snug Harbor.

BUZZARD ISLAND

A frieze of naked limbs, gaunt, sinister,
Against the sanguine anguish of the west.
No sound except the steady cluck and purr
Of thirsty streams that tap the sky's bared breast,
And crawl through blind canals until they flood
The barren levels of the empty fields,
The fallen dikes, the rotting trunks with blood.

Now, as the fading horror swoons tonight,
Like cinders scattered from a funeral pyre,
Coursing and veering in the upper light,
With bellies ruddy from the ebbing fire,
The vultures circle down until their breath
Poisons the stagnant air, until the stark
Awaiting trees blossom and leaf with death.

Beyond these rice-fields and their crawling streams,
Young voices ring; white cities lift and spread.
This is the rookery of still-born dreams;

NOTE: Buzzard Island is a buzzard rookery among abandoned
rice-fields on the coast of South Carolina.

Here old faiths gather after they are dead,
Outlived despairs slant by on evil wing,
And bitter memories that time has starved
Home down the closing dusk for comforting.

THE EQUINOX

Heavy with salt, and warm,
And damp from the Caribbean,
Like a wrestler's body
Muscled under its sweat;
Sounding a deep alarm
That shrills to a pæan,
It charges the shuddering spit
Where the rivers have met.

Under its whirling cloak
The hummocks and houses are shrunken
To figures of fear
In the blue-green daylight-dark.
Only a dwarfed sea-oak
Leans truculent, drunken,
Brandishing terrible arms
That wind-bludgeons leave stark.

From the demoniac vault
Gargantuan sledges
Crash to the huddling roofs

Until frail timbers start.
Then thundering to the assault
Like surf on the ledges,
The weight of the wind drives through
And rends them apart.

Now the palmettoes that lash
On the southern-most beaches
Thrill to the shout of the storm
And sing through the rain.
Remembering typhoons that smash
Along tropical reaches,
They batter the winds with great hands,
And are happy again.

CHANT FOR AN OLD TOWN

Builders of high white towers in the sun;
Masters, yet driven by the force you spend;
Can you not feel beneath the soil you rend
A surer rhythm than you have yet begun:
The drum of steady pulses that have done
With stone and iron, colors, and the bend
Of certain beauty; workers, friend and friend,
Whose hands wrought slowly until grace was won.

Trading new lamps for old, you storm the street.
Then, heedless of the magic in the old,
You leave them strewn in fragments at our gate.
Oh, pause before the ruin is complete.
For that which stands have pity, and withhold.
Leave for your sons these walls inviolate.

1

It has been told above the fading embers
That once beneath a cloud-wracked, frightened
    moon,

61

When the Governor's ships drove down upon the
    pirates,
And days were numbered for the picaroon,
A long-boat swept from sea toward the city,
Slender, and dark, and eager as a sword,
Cleaving the swirling play of light and shadow
That made the bay a crazy checker-board.

And once the light drenched down and limned a
    picture
That caused the blood to stagger, hang, and freeze;
For the boat leapt clear, and in the stern sat Black-
    beard
Nursing a bloody cutlass on his knees.

And the watchers paled and shifted in the dark-
    ness,
Hugging the shadows when the moon flared
    through;
For the ships were out, and gaunt below the city
Stood gibbets that had swung a pirate crew;
While a Judas wind went whispering among them,
And bent palmettoes muttered all they knew.

But the drone of parted water never slackened.
The splash of oars and tumble of the wake
Dwindled and ebbed along the windy river,

And died at the city's edge where forests break.
And silence fluttered back from the hidden
    marshes,
Throbbed, and bore upon them like an ache.

But the negroes tell of a silent landing-party
That hacked a path through tangled scrub and
    vine,
And a long-boat beached where greying live-oaks
    crowded
About a creek to dabble their beards in brine.
Of a sullen torch that splashed vermillion patches
On a face from Hell, and sweat upon the backs
Of diggers working heavily in silence;
And a chest borne down by two great straining
    blacks
Into a yawning hole. Then color of fire
Poured from a sudden blade to the stooping men
Terribly cleaving souls from splendid bodies;
And a voice: "Guard well until I come again."

Darkness then, and the heavy rhythmic thudding
Of sods on wood and the flesh of those on guard;
A hush that built about them slowly, stilling
Even a distant pulse where tholepins jarred.

2

A gust of years went by, and then the blowing
Of steady decades kind to a new land.
Like a spent storm, the head of Blackbeard
    glowered
Through rainbows at a frigate's prow, while sand
And the terrible strong teeth of deep-sea hunters
Fretted the tarnished cutlass from his hand.

Streets spread, and quiet forest paths receded.
Men built with hands that loved the feel of stone,
And hearts that knew elusive ways of Beauty,
Who mates a loving touch—or lives alone.
Where forests fell the grateful soil reflowered
In slender portico and stuccoed wall.
Old stones from France lay in the narrow drive-
    ways,
And through their crevices the many small
Sweet fingers of the Spring would lift un-
    hindered.
Summer would mount there like a tropic wave
Spilling pomegranate coral through the gardens.
There figs, seapurple, ripened, and the brave
Old tattered banners of bananas fluttered
About their heavy fruit. White mornings sprawled

64

On wharves that loved the bay, where chanties
    rang;
And August courtyards, flagged and lichen-walled,
Where negroes bought and sold, and laughed and
    sang.
Above deep streets hung weathered copper spires
And domes to take the sun, and, like a crowd
Of patient watchers over fading splendors,
High toppling dormers, staring shaggy-browed.
Cowled doorways bore the chisel's mark upon them,
And iron-work in many a harp and scroll,
Beaten by hands that shaped red yielding metal,
Still bore the fleeting imprint of a soul.

But there are things that human clay may handle,
And warm its coldness on, and speed its breath
For one brief day. Then, like a flaring candle,
They go. Beauty is such. The seed of death
Is born in lovely things to ripen slowly
And kill them before we are satisfied.
Only the dead are free to give up wholly,
And follow mortal beauty that has died.

3

The engines come.
Through the short night

65

They breathe their iron breathing,
Waiting the dawn.
Then *snarl*, and
           SHATTER, SHATTER, SHATTER!
"Frail city of hands,
What have you to offer?
Can you prove by mathematics
Why you should survive?
Pierced by plunging caissons,
Walled by towering concrete;
What have you to compare
With the superb accuracy
Of a blue-print,
Or the relentless convergence
Of a studied perspective?
Can you give us a sea-wall
Like that of Buenos Aires,
Or a hotel the mate to twenty others
In great American cities?
A hundred Western towns say you are wrong;
And in answer
You smile your faded, wistful smile,
And show us a crooked, moss-hung tree
A century old;
And the way a street

66

Bends a protecting arm
About an impossible curve.

SHATTER, SHATTER, SHATTER!

See how a house can climb
Sheer to the zenith,
Floor hurled upon floor,
While the girders swing dizzily upward.
We show you a street like
Pennsylvania Avenue,
Canal Street,
Riverside Drive,
All asphalt and uniform concrete.
And you dodder of ancient flagged pave-
*   ments*
That lay like faint pastel mosaics
Between careless gardens
That were like nothing else upon Earth.

SHATTER, SHATTER, SHATTER!

Ah, you are silent at last."

4

Under the feet of a tall machine,
In the false and tricky dark
That grew where the sky-flung derricks lean
Over the littered park,

A gang of negroes burrowing
With bar, and pick, and spade,
Tugged and bent to an iron ring
In a hole their tools had made.

A sudden give, and the earth fell clear,
A gasp, and seven blacks
Bunched and cringed, and muttered a prayer
To the thing behind their backs.

For a moon grown suddenly old and blue
Laid withered hands upon
A mouldy chest, and a bone or two
From a rotting skeleton;

A shooting-star whined overhead,
The arc-lights winced and failed,
And a lonely wind from the longtime dead
Crept to their ears and wailed.

Then Terror loosed them, and let them go
In a storm of flailing feet,
To tell their tale by the lantern glow
Of the shops in Sailor Street.

But when the engines summoned day
Up from oblivion,
And the gang crept back to loot the clay,
The chest and the bones were gone.

Simon, the drunkard, swears he saw them going,
In a shaking world of neither-here-nor-there,
Tottering out of the shades, and slowly blowing
Across the park, lighter than harbor air,
With a wedge of the milky-way serenely showing
Through cloven skulls under the matted hair.

Yes, he will tell you that he watched them travel
Out to the city's edge with a mouldy chest.
How they would bulk in the dark, and then unravel
Under the lights. And when they paused to rest,
Dusted their burden free of city gravel,
And waited tense, lest any should molest.

Heaving their treasure to their backs, they waded
The last salt stream, and, where the forests keep
The old lost darks and silences, they faded.

＊　＊　＊　＊　＊　＊　＊

Back in the early grey, steel-throated, deep,
The engines ripped the silence, and the jaded,
Driven city stumbled from its sleep.

Envoy

So, at the last, I think that we must follow,
When Death has struck us free to dream and rest;
When the great engines rock the world about us,

And sow bright, bitter cities down the West.
Then we may go, we who guarded Beauty
Hidden from eyes that were not taught to see,
Out to the city's edge, in the covering night-time,
Bearing a ghostly treasure secretly.
And those who meet us in the echoing silence
Will neither challenge us nor stay our pace.
For our shimmering store would fetch no silver
Under the sun in any market-place.
Only the sky will know us, and the silence,
And the great cloud-leviathans that spawn
Their sullen young beyond the smoking marshes
To range the painted ocean of the dawn.
Time will flow by us then like a wide blue river.
But we will never heed its steady pull,
Nor mourn the tragic freightage that it carries,
Broken, but beautiful.
We will hold fast against the crowding shadows,
Late and soon,
Beauties that breath built tenderly at sunrise,
To fade at noon.
These we will hoard, and treasure, and remember;
Waiting dead captains who will never come,
Statesmen, and dreamers, workers with taut sinews,
Who builded Beauty here, and called it *home*.

RETURN

The spent day dwindles west along the strand.
Wide-ranging sea-winds veer and circle home,
Trailing slow pinions, luminous where foam
Breaks to their touch. Now the last gust of sand
Goes stinging by; and where the myrtles stand,
Wind-shorn and huddled in the lee of dunes,
The sleepy wings bruise leaves till evening
    swoons
With drowsy perfume, and sleep folds the land.

So I would come again where loved things are,
An æon hence, after my voyaging.
When I have tired of the last wild star
And winds set homeward, I would turn and
    fling
My length beside these dunes, and know again
The night's deep solace, and the myrtle's pain.

Other Poems

YOUR GIFTS

You could not give me toys in those bleak days;
So when my playmates proudly boasted theirs,
You caught me to the shelter of your arms,
And taught me how to laugh away my tears.
Having no books, you sang a shining word
Into my open palm, and closed it tight.
And some far God of Little Children heard,
And gave you of His best for my delight.
So, when the neighbors' children shouted by,
Their hired nurse-maids herding them like
    sheep;
Then, that old dauntless look of yours would
    leap,
And, leading me beneath the western skies,
You woke their mirrored glory in my eyes.

And there were nights; do you remember still.
Forgetting playthings we could never buy,

We journeyed out beyond the farthest hill,
Adventuring along the evening sky,
And you would teach the meaning of the stars.
Not the dull purpose vaguely guessed by sages,
And catalogued in musty study-books,
But wild, fantastic legends of lost ages,
That none but their Creator ever knew,
And that He whispered only once to one
Frail, lonely mother—and that mother—you.

Now autumn years are blowing swiftly by,
And I come empty-handed from my quest;
Save for a captured wraith of sunset sky,
A star or two, and last and loveliest,
The little shining word you gave to me:
Treasures no human hand may ever hold.
But you first knew their wonder and their
    worth;
You who have made me rich with more than
    gold.

74

CREATION

(A soldier speaks)

There is a holiness upon her as she waits
Close by the station gates.
All of the forenoon long
Hastens the restless throng;
Eyes that seem scarcely to live,
Faces with nothing to give,
Swung by the rock of the years
On to their narrow affairs.

Now women come who draw their skirts aside;
And negro porters, braced against the tide
Of beating life, shrug with a smile or sneer
Seeing her waiting there.

Where the massed shadows crawl
Out from the soaring wall
Her face shows drawn and small.
Only her eyes,
Somber, remote, and wise,
Gaze out of æons past

75

Over today to the vast
Dream of tomorrow.
All of Earth's sorrow
Lies there, and all of Earth's joy;
And the infinite patience that builds
While armies destroy.

These others who beat in a tide
Of turbulent life through the wide
High gate,
Perhaps they go seeking their fate.
She needs but to wait.

What has she to do with the strife!
Her concern is of life,
Faint-stirring and small,
Biding its time till the call
Of the earth for its child
Out of its night, to the wild
Glad urge of its day;
So, while they go on their way,
She can wait
By the gate.

And I, who make of my brain, and my soul, and
my hand,
Only a driven machine to depeople a land,

Turn, as the blind must turn to the warmth of the
      sun,
Toward one
Who mutely and steadfastly, up from the night and
      the sod,
Is shaping a life in the wonderful likeness of God.

ELEGY

They are so sure of you now,
The loving and cruel and blind.
You are so frail and small
Since the light dimmed out of your face.
Death's ultimate commonplace
Has given you back to them all:
Now they can comprehend
And afford to be kind.

You are so plastic now;
So submissive and still.
Your slender, rebellious hands
Have been folded and hidden away.
You, who were too brave to pray
When your soul was scarred by the bands
That they forged through the years
On your youth, and your dream, and your
    will.

They can be generous now,
They who never have given.

When they gave you a shaft
Complacently branded "At Rest,"
I think that you paused in your quest
Worlds away, while you laughed
Your old dauntless laugh
Through your startled new Heaven.

MILESTONES

Once, in a darkened crowd,
I heard you laugh;
And for a moment, once
I saw you flare
Warm in the eyes of a friend;
But when the lights went up,
And when I looked again,
You were not there.
Children have touched me often
With your hands.
Death brought you to my bedside
One black day,
And, with the lips of an old, sad woman
You kissed me twice;
But, when I groped for you
You went away.
Now, while long evening hills
Ride down the west,
Like caravans of opal
Sunset bound,

Pulling the dusty dark along the dew;
Million-tongued and strange,
You summon me.
And I must quench my fire,
And follow you.

ALTERNATIVES

Oh, Time will break us as he has the others.
The beautiful and strong, the gay, the proud,
Between the cradling breasts of their two mothers
Have sung their weary hearts out to the crowd.
Rich in a metal that no mint may utter,
They struck hot, molten youth into a song;
And, with it, won the solace of the gutter—
Villon, and Poe, and all the lonely throng.

And here today, while our own songs, unsung,
Still hum, pent fire, in our quick arteries;
While the sweet agony of being young
Is ours, and this pollen-heavy breeze
Has loosed your hair, and fanned a sudden flame,
I wonder so—I falter on your name.

INTERLUDE

Breathe very gently now, and you can feel it
Stirring between our palms, reluctant to stay.
See, they have passed in the storm, and their lan-
     terns are fading.
Now it is ours until the dawn takes it away.

Close your eyes tightly now, in the veiled star-
     light—
Eyes that have learned to see too cruelly clear.
Only the blind are wise: our fingers may slacken;
Then, if we look, we may find but emptiness there.
Press very closely now, that we may hold it
Between our hearts. See, the darkness blooms sud-
     denly warm.
When we awake our hands will be open and empty.
Then, seeker and dreamer again, we will bend to
     the storm.

TWO POEMS

1

APRIL

When we are older
We can be tender.
Now, with the splendor
Of April about us,
While we are bolder
Than our doubters,
There is a planet
I must acquire
Before they can ban it.
While this swift fire
Leaps in your laughter,
You must be after
Your moon.
　　　　　In November
We will be older,
Sadder—colder;
Then we'll remember
Your head, and my shoulder.

84

NOVEMBER

I could forget your face,
And the slow gathering comfort of your smile.
The cold white fire of your slender hand
Kept me remembering a little while,
But there was much to know and understand,
To puzzle out and trace.

I could even forget the way
You laughed and tossed your head to hide the pain
That April morning when you let me go.
Strong with the strength to conquer heart with
    brain,
I crushed you swiftly out; and did not know
That I must ever pay.

I should not have come
Back to these dunes and sky that never alter,
The sweeping condemnation of this sea
We loved together. Here at last I falter,
Tortured and broken by the constancy
Of things unknowing, dumb.

NEW ENGLAND LANDSCAPE

On a sepia ground
Shot with orange light,
The pines,
In blue-black lines,
And birches, slender,
Diagonal, and white,
Stencil compact designs.
The inevitable wall,
As it leaves the woods,
Breaks to a sprawl
Of separate stones
Echoing the tones
Of sepia and orange
With high lights
Of chrome and red,
Until they find a bed
In the splotched lilac
Of the meadow,
Or chill to blue in shadow.
In the valley's cupped palm

Lies a handful of ripening grain.
And, riding the high blue calm
Over Monadnock,
A decorous cloud
Is slowly unwinding its skein.

MATINS

I saw you pray today
Out in the park,
Storm-driven child
Of the nethermost dark.

Body to earth you lay
On the young grass,
Learning the shining way
April may pass.

I saw the clear song
Cardinals make
Brush your face tangibly
Like wind on the lake.

Then, in the hedge
Where japonicas grew,
A little breeze was born,
Boyish and new.

I saw it find you
And rustle your name;

Lift you, and carry you
Like a slim flame

Out where the trees break,
Leaving wide skies.
Now I see always
The prayer in your eyes.

41648

SPRING MOOD

I cannot bear the park today;
The children, and the sad old men on benches;
Spring greedily devouring decay
That was an Autumn,
Generous, and passionate, and strong;
A sun too cruel-bright, that drenches
The little walled-in square,
And nurtures buoyant hope
On energy it draws from old despair.
Bright waves of children break about the old,
Laugh, and recede more joyous than they
    came.
The sitters on the benches
Stir and shift uneasily,
Cackle, scold,
And dwindle visibly.

A callous wind
Hums a gay stave or two,
Then brooms a whirl of leaves.

Helpless, they circle, mutter, and subside.
Like tongues of flame,
Young grass leaps flickering through.

And suddenly the mask slips.
Under the color and the sun,
The hideous, irrevocable plan
Works nakedly.
Youth, with its lips
Red from the carcasses of age,
Now, as when time began,
Makes of the quiet square a charnel cage.

Tomorrow I may love my park again.
Now, I must get hence, and be alone
Among the shouldering millions,
To breathe where man entrenches
Himself with gods and stone
To shut out death.
I cannot bear the park today;
The children, and the sad old men on benches.

AUTUMN MOOD

Summer, come home.
Wreckage of crimson and chrome
On your moist green floor of mosses . . .
Sunlight that Autumn has turned
From copper to brass
Thrusting slim bars through the dome
That October has shattered
And spurned.
The fragile, intricate house
That you reared for your reticent soul
Is open and battered,
Shaken in beam, and in rafter;
Nothing is whole.
See in the cynical light
The tale of your losses.
Winds lift ironical laughter.
Nothing has mattered.
Come home.

WEARINESS

I do not dread the coming of Old Age:
I am so tired today—so wholly spent.
Kind hands are suddenly belligerent.
"If you lack strength to earn your daily wage,
Give us your soul," they cry, "your heritage
Of pride." Revengeful winds that I have bent
Before my body's strength, finding me impotent,
Lash me to cover with their blinding rage.

Now, if the form that I have always feared
Should take my nerveless hand, and, like a
    friend,
Say "Come and rest a while. Forget the mad
And futile fight—the thinking that you cared—
The shout—the kiss. Come, dream until the end
Here with me in the sun," I could be glad.

AFTERMATH

TO EDWARD L. WELLS. KILLED IN ACTION.

When, in the darkest hour of our dark night,
You took the sum of all you had to give,
Your splendid body, with its right to live,
Your soaring mind, with all its latent might,
And hurled it with a shout into the fight;
I could have wept that you would never see
The triumph of the dream that seemed to be
Upon you and about you like a light.

Now, while our boastful triumph shakes the
    dawn,
Revenge and greed have cast their cloaks aside,
The people perish, and we waste our breath;
All those who dared to dream are laughed to
    scorn,
While, one by one, their dreams are crucified:
Almost I envy you your rich, young death.

94

PRODIGAL

Some day when the stern seeker in my brain
Has ceased to drive me stumbling through the
     dark
Dropping dead cinders for each faint new spark,
Only to see the new one wax and wane.
When all my dreams are numbered with the slain,
And Wisdom, that egregious Patriarch,
Has told his last half truth, and left me stark,
I shall go home. I shall go home again.

Friendship will greet me in the panelled hall,
And Laughter will enfold me on the stairs
Sweet as old rose leaves wrinkled in a jar.
Battles and loves will move me not at all.
There will be juleps, billiards, family prayers,
And a calm crossing to another star.

EPITAPH FOR A POET

Here lies a spendthrift who believed
That only those who spend may keep;
Who scattered seeds, yet never grieved
Because a stranger came to reap;

A failure who might well have risen;
Yet, ragged, sang exultantly
That all success is but a prison,
And only those who fail are free:

Who took what little Earth had given,
And watched it blaze, and watched it die;
Who could not see a distant Heaven
Because of dazzling nearer sky;

Who never flinched till Earth had taken
The most of him back home again,
And the last silences were shaken
With songs too lovely for his pen.